Some Girls Survive on Their Sorcery Alone

Some Girls Survive on Their Sorcery Alone

Poems

Thiahera Nurse

NORTHWESTERN UNIVERSITY PRESS

EVANSTON, ILLINOIS

Northwestern University Press
www.nupress.northwestern.edu

Northwestern University Poetry and Poetics Colloquium
www.poetry.northwestern.edu

Printed in the United States of America

10 9 8 7 6 5 4 3 2 1

Library of Congress Cataloging-in-Publication Data
Names: Nurse, Thiahera, author. | Gibbons, Reginald, writer of foreword.
Title: Some girls survive on their sorcery alone : poems / Thiahera Nurse.
Other titles: Drinking gourd chapbook poetry prize.
Description: Evanston, Illinois : Northwestern University Press, 2019. | Series: Drinking
gourd chapbook poetry prize
Identifiers: LCCN 2018036960 | ISBN 9780810140196 (pbk. : alk. paper)
Subjects: LCSH: African Americans—Social conditions—Poetry.
Classification: LCC PS3614.U866 A6 2019 | DDC 811.6—dc23
LC record available at https://lccn.loc.gov/2018036960

For Geo

Contents

Foreword

Reginald Gibbons

Thiahera Nurse writes that she is "running hard, fast, and away from elegy."
But with the tremendously vigorous energy of her language she runs right
at danger, pain, suffering, and heartache. In her poems, vulnerability to
others' strength, subjection to others' power, racism, and a defense of
one's own sexual integrity are vivid, threatening realities. She defeats such
hazards by articulating them in dazzling images and metaphors.

With utter frankness, brilliant defiance, and compelling heartbreak,
Nurse brings to the reader the most wrenching experiences and the most
vital determination to survive, to flout danger and pain and even to spite
them, at least for a while, with imagination and verbally inventive fierce-
ness. These poems articulate bravery, sassing even against dangers to body
and soul. Sexual danger is frequently portrayed: Nurse writes of walking
with a homegirl, both of them in suede dresses, against a human current
"fiending and fawning // at the wedge of our black stiletto heels."

In a prose poem, Nurse writes, "She had a slick mouth. When she
spoke, gasoline and cod liver oil flushed out of her smooth as velvet.
He could not walk by without her saying impossibly wild shit about his
shoes, his mama, the shirt he wore when the iron ran cold. No one could
out-shit-talk that blk girl with the sharp slits in her face for eyes."

Mortal risks are the context of these poems. Also, the mortal thrills of
defying those risks. Images of profound resignation, such as "I breathe in
the ocean, and she clears / my birth canal into a sacred grave," do not rule
out scenes of momentary audacity, as when Nurse writes, about young
women who revenge-key a rapist's silver car, "We laugh belly first. We
howl at the silver-slick moon."

After young women have helped a teenage girl survive, honoring her as
if her pain, fear, and abjection had made her a saint of lamentably every-

day suffering, Nurse writes of the young women around the girl, "Horse mouths bowed / to the good water." Nurse's images of suffering can be powerful shocks: "The medicine grated at me until my insides were minced." These are poems of both damage and courage. "God cut the first / wound in the earth and called it 'the sky.' I am learning // blood comes from all over."

"Noah did not know who Jesus was but a storm / was coming and he was black, so he had to believe. // This is about staying alive." Nurse writes, "I have been at the mercy of another girl's musings and / cruel examinations"—and other poems tell of being at the mercy of dangerous men. Brave and resolute, she says of herself and others, "we are girls and ready to ride- / or-die."

Thiahera Nurse encompasses an extraordinary range of experience and feeling. With her splendid, rousing, expressive powers, she draws us into the visionary fervor of her remarkable engagement with life and language.

Some Girls Survive on Their Sorcery Alone

Some Girls Survive on Their Sorcery Alone

I got a stank-ass attitude
because you tried to kill me.
Still, I am the baddest bitch in here.

Diamond yoni. Carbon-based funk and it's everywhere.
Video vixen-bad. Thick with the stuff my mama gave me,
her mama gave her. It's cyclical, this survival. My gap-toothed gait
    bending
the corner. Bow-legged Athena, if this story needed a white goddess
    to exist.
Let me compare myself to my black-ass self:

a stillborn summer=roadkill=every deer gnawed through=peepholes
where my breasts should be

How easy it is to eat through the faces
of black girls with your weapons.
A flesh that don't crack
and yet—

> Here I am. My bottom lip split down
> the middle. You save the fat you want
> for yourselves. Your daughters pickle my
> mouth in a jar they keep on the nightstand.

What did slavery do to y'all
to make you treat me this way?
I almost wonder and then I am
distracted by my own brilliance.

Pink lotion slides down the side of my neck,
        I'm sweating—running hard, fast, and away from elegy.

If I die in this jail cell, no, I did not kill myself. If I die in this jail cell, no, I did not kill myself.
If I die in this jail cell, no, I did not kill myself. If I die in this jail cell, no, I did not kill myself.

For **Sandra Bland Aiyanna Mo'nay Stanley-Jones Renisha McBride Reese Walker Tarika Wilson Kathryn Johnson Sherese Francis Korryn Gaines** and nem.

> [The understood, implicit et cetera of this list.]

I am trying to mend the impossible wound and I seal it
in cocoa butter. I'm blasting Lil' Kim in the rain. So much
coconut oil on me, the bullets miss. I'm slick as fuck.
You mad you can still smell me breathing from here?

In Defense of Injury: A Hex

In Fatima's attic, we decide that keying
Darius's car is the appropriate response.
Though we are brave enough to murder, we do not.
Fatima holds her black eye like a jewel.

She means to pass us the organ gleaming from her face
as it bling-blings from the torn socket. Fatima sits
at the center of our healing circle in defense of her injuries.

She runs back the story

of her Tuesday night, and our gums
wail against our teeth. She loses so much blood a baby
unhinges itself from the floor. Her face creaking open
like the door Darius snatches with his ash-blue knuckles,
his motherfucking fists.

This is about revenge, about reciprocity.
Me and my girls are obsessed with getting even
because we remember the times when we were not brave.
It felt like a scalp being upturned in soil. Crotchet braids ripped
clean from Fatima's roots by a boy's nimble wrist.

God, make me white so that I may beat Darius's ass
in front of the police. God, this is the Olde English speaking.
A bad attitude steeped in malt liquor and rum. We take turns.
We kiss Fatima's black eye until it is her black eye, again.

Who would give us a loaded gun in a time of war? We could slit a throat
with what we use to unlock our mothers' doors. That's a prayer,
I think. And then we bowed to Darius's machine dripping in candy paint.
Sliced the hood until we snap the platinum metal meat. When the keys
    dull,

we used the blade of our acrylic nails. Synthetic, as in the moment felt unreal.

Our lungs hot. 40-proof. We laugh belly first. We howl at the silver-slick moon.

Pain Is Love

for the late Foster Laurie Police Athletic League on 112th Avenue

for V.

for Ja Rule

Ja Rule's voice pours through the roof of the PAL gymnasium like rain
and we understand that yes, *pain is love*. The speakers line the stage like black
coffins // like black roaches stacked on the backs of black roaches.

Valentina's gold chain bucks against the beat. Her neck leans
on a swivel as she raps "Always On Time" like the words to the Our Father.
She writes Ja's name in black Sharpie through the center pleat of her plaid skirt.

She crosses herself in three directions at the end of every verse.
The winter of 2001 came with a Parental Advisory sticker tucked inside
her dark blue mouth. We wore the losses. We were the wounds and the wounded.

My brown arms made black and blue by the metal rings
of the swizzle stick held in my mother's hand. Valentina's thick braids
yanked from her head like the spine of many weeds.

Her skin pulping through the fine veil of her hair.
Small pools of blood line the edge of her forehead. I kiss the holes
where her baby-hair used to be. In my mouth, a snatch of daffodil buds.

In my mouth, a block of banana Laffy Taffys Valentina copped me from
Hollis Deli.

My favorite, I say with a yellow throat to the brown girl. I kiss the last
   candy.
I keep them safe in my book bag for later.

I press small scoops of Vaseline above Valentina's scarred
brow with my purple fingers. 2001 and her deep dark mouth.
Me and Valentina peeling underneath fluorescent light.

Beneath the wooden floorboards of a repurposed Catholic school
on 112th Avenue, we praised who we knew would save us: the Ja-voiced
   miracle.
His voice eaten by gravel. Baritone sifted through sand.

*Always there when you call (BUCKSHOTS HA!) / always on time / always
on time / always there when you always / always on time / always there when
you / always / always /always.*

We laugh hard with our taffy throats. Our lips thick with gloss,
heavy with the bruises our mothers gave us: *pain is love pain is love*
the tattoo over Ja's heart reminding us of the blood we came from.

**Granny Juanita Is Dead—I Come to Her Funeral Wearing a
White Dress and an Overnight Diaper**

I bleed through the pew, anyway.
A line the color of rust aches down the seam of my stockings.

My stockings the color of gauze. Gauze clogs the wound
that is my vagina. My mother is worried about how long

this period is running through me. Running me straight
to the ground, where my Granny stay now. Say now:

the doctors gut the child out of me like a school of flying fish.
Been bleeding ever since—like I don't have any home training:

I lie to my mother in the House of the Lord. She wonders
about the clots, round as the small knobs on my grandmother's front
    door.

My feet swollen to the size of my father's great fists. My grandmother's
    mouth
in a golden coffin: stained-glass-window crimson. Her perfect face

gleaming out from the casket like a coin. God can flip
any hex into a hymn, into a prayer I can sing into myself

in the hour of my death. I hold my rosary beads close
to my chest. I must be cursed. Miscarrying as they bend

my granny's body through the flame. God reminding me
of the Hell from which I came. Her ashes folded into the earth

and through the Caribbean Sea. I breathe in the ocean, and she clears
my birth canal into a sacred grave. Poinsettias blooming

from the former cave. I mean to say that this poem is about
my Granny Juanita and me—the Hail Marys we sang,

though we were not saved. Two dead girls wearing lipstick
the color of rubies on the day God called us home.

Love and Water

after Nabila Lovelace

I am just like anyone else, I need love and water.

                              —Prince

Never stay with the man who fucks you
and does not keep water in his refrigerator.
Cotton mouth latched to the tap in a silver kitchen.

How original. You are thirsty and your pussy
is wet. Even that is a failing. You suck the valve until
every pipe in the city is dry, and somehow you are

the one left rusting from the inside out. Like everyone
else, you need love and water to survive. And which
can he give to you? His cum so damp and stagnant,

silverfish grow between your tired legs. A nerve
in your tooth browning the moment he pulls out.
Your pussy is so good, and you know it. But even

good can be improved. Perhaps you did not
give your best. Maybe you didn't fry the chicken
hard enough. He chewed the tacky meat and

was unimpressed. It is possible that when
you called him *daddy*, he remembered the abortion
and was disgusted by you, all over again.

And still you begged him to stay, until you sweated out
your perm. All that lye in his sheets making the bedroom
smell like a human scalp was burning. It was.

Ode to Being Late

We show up four minutes late to first period gym and
Mr. B gives us two demerits each. Blows his whistle.
Makes us run three miles with no water. Asks how early
we have to get up just to get *here* late. Says we should talk.
We wait near his office by the vending machines. We share a Honey Bun
between three sets of red fingers. Our nails clink together like glass.
Strange cake raked against the roof of my mouth. Sweetness on the
    tongue,
thick as blue grease. He says, You and your friends are always *late*. Says
    late like
someone he owns just walked into the room. I remember how everyone
    says
Mr. B is a down-ass white boy. *The three of y'all—late. Walking in here like
    TLC.*
A joke is made by a down-ass white boy with a whistle, which is to say
    our laughter
must have sounded like *yes, yes, yes* through the walls. Even if we had said
    no,
who would have heard us? We were so close to the boiler room. Our
    voices
must have been pressed thin by steam. It was a basement. My body, I
    mean.
The way I saved his tongue inside of me like a little trauma I could even-
    tually forget
locked away in a damp room.

Web

What I know of betrayal, I learn from the holes in my own body.
Each one a mouth opening and stinking of iron. I was a girl when

I learned to clot myself with cotton and fingernails. Fistula caking
the flora of panties. Muddy mire streaming the length of a thigh.

For days I avoided soap and water, and even the flies dropped
their eggs in my ears. The maggotry of raping the girl-child so stank,

she stains herself. A stripped mattress and the tongue in my dead head,
slipping past the raw throat. O, stigmata cackling in the pit of my palm.

O gentle Jesus, meek and mild. The sight of blood that interrupts nothing
but the shade of the room. Eggshell easy splintering. Yolk running down
   my chin.

I stick to myself, and wonder who will throw away the mouse on the glue
   trap.
The corners of the room littered with spiders. If only God was kind, He
   would

make me a small, productive insect. I would watch the girl gagging
on the bed and continue to work and wait until food flew into her web—
   into my mouth.

Leanna

Leanna presses the head of a Barbie between
my legs and I swell at the center. She asks if it hurts.
I say nothing as she rips me apart. I am a mouthless

doll. Slow cotton lifting from my cloth chest. Yes,
I am torn in two and I do not scream. My whole life,

I have been at the mercy of another girl's musings and
cruel examinations. I was small, easy to keep a secret
inside of my blood-honed mouth.
My limp waist creaking against their palms.
My body purpling in rage. The floorboard cawing
at the underbelly of the girlish bed.

I love you Jesus, I love you Jesus.

and He never comes to get me. [I just want to be gathered.]

Yes, I was torn in two and was told
not to scream. The shushing of my name
lulling me into deadpan slumber with the bald head
of a Barbie corking me until I bled.

Go with God

Go with God. God is all-knowing. God cut the first
wound in the earth and called it "the sky." I am learning

blood comes from all over. There isn't a window in my body I
haven't closed. I need air. I can't breathe. There was oxygen,

and then there was nothing at all. The room boiling, like hell.
I know the labor of slipping into my own ghost. But I wanted to

live, so I imagined a god. He would clean me with soap and steam.
The holes in my head sopped up, and fixed. I imagined a peace only

bloodlessness could bring. I called for God. My throat peeled
raw until bleating, until wild, unrefined stone seed. This is the

animal I am. I am calling a sacrificial attention to myself.
My stomach blooming in lamb's blood. A boy pushes a pair of

knees into the mattress. I curse the inventor
of this room, of my crushable bones.

Mesh

I am trying desperately to avoid the blood of others
and I end up closer to myself in the poem every time.

I write down the name of every dead thing in this room
so that I know which of you are my ghosts. The list is long

with every word you've ever called me in the dark. Praise my mother
and her penchant for gold—the nameplate hanging off my neck

like a cowbell. I announce myself as the only animal in the room.
How could I forget who and what I belong to? I cock my head

back against the pillow, and there is a sound like a gong that goes off
in my head when you fuck me. You lean in and thin the music

with your mouth and unoriginal questions. You ask whose pussy this is
because you know I can lie. There goes that blood again and you don't
  notice.

I am lying through my fucking teeth. I can't tell if you make me dead
  inside,
or if I came here this way. I don't know what to do when the funeral fails

at allegory and is so literal I dress for it and it is called lingerie.
My breasts falling out of a lace cage, my skin splitting like mesh.

Chase Does Not Eat Black Pussy

Chase does not eat black pussy. Chase only reads Du Bois. Chase is
getting his Ph.D. in blackness. Chase is dating a white girl from New
Mexico, now. New Mexican White Girl–Pussy leaks bleach. Chase eats
white pussy until his insides are scraped clean. Chase keeps blond pubic
hairs under his retainer. Chase is a collector. Chase collects. Chase does
not eat black pussy. Chase fucked me in his apartment in Not-New
Mexico. Chase did not eat my pussy. My pussy can't pass for white.
My pussy is not a part of the talented tenth. Chase fucked me and
was displeased. My pussy hasn't read enough books. My pussy is not
concerned with building a black middle class. Chase has Ivy League dick.
Chase has dreams. Chase wants green-eyed infants with good hair. Chase
has valuable sperm. Chase keeps bleach all over his apartment. Chase
inhales Clorox and gets hard. Chase did not make me cum. Chase came,
only in my mouth. Chase sterilized my teeth. Chase cleaned—

slickmouth

She had a slick mouth. When she spoke, gasoline and cod liver oil flushed out of her smooth as velvet. He could not walk by without her saying impossibly wild shit about his shoes, his mama, the shirt he wore when the iron ran cold. No one could out-shit-talk that blk girl with the sharp slits in her face for eyes. One time she blinked too fast and he caught a buck fifty across the face. *Why is you bleeding*, she'd say as she used that tar-slick mouth to mend his cuts like warm asphalt on an unpaved road. After she nursed the wounds, she'd fix her mouth into petals all over his back and neck. The aged augite of his flesh rolled over her own, and she felt like she could make love to this man for as long as the sun steeped itself through the earth. They'd lie on the water-stained mattress and she would hum songs she heard on the radio right through his sleeping chest. She rapped Method Man's verse off "You're All I Need" thirty-two times as he snored, his breathing tuned to the meter of a honeybee. The day she saw her lover decaying on the street like four-hour-old roadkill, her narrow eyes pulled dry as a razor blade. She watched the caution tape strung like Christmas lights all around his blk, and almost blue, body. The girl tried to fix that slick mouth to say something foul and smart-assed. But he just lay there, bled out like he had no home training. She screamed his name and every white face looked right through her. Like she wasn't speaking the Queen's English. Like the boy she loved wasn't even real. Isn't that what being a blk girl is all about? Letting the boy you made strong disappear at the hiss of a bullet, knowing that he is a temporary sweetness that your mouth cannot laminate with teflon? Then you are over his body smackin' your gums, swinging your neck, wondering why the sound of your voice isn't making him get his blk ass up?

**Raw Video Footage: A Year after the Shooting McBride's Family
Asks for Peace—Joe Biden Holds an Ice Cream Cone**

Getting shot in the face turns
the girl into a dog. The internet says
Renisha knocks loudly on Theodore Wafer's
windows and doors. That is a mistake.

He sends an end-stopped bullet
through her cheek, so clean it feels
conversational. A year later, he googles this
part of himself. Maybe he's eating ice cream.

That delicious porch in Dearborn Heights
spreads its glucose across his teeth—
parts her scalp across the street.

He watches YouTube footage of the Detroit vigil—
He shot my niece down like she was a dog.

The hind legs of Renisha's plasma rear off
the asphalt, and on the right side of his screen
Joe Biden is being polled on America's

favorite ice cream flavor. *Rocky road rocky road
rocky road*—his pink chin splitting through
chocolate, black spit.

Ice cream is good   years after   the expiration date
all you need is a   *solid freezer.*

Theodore eats his weight in dairy.
His dog Lightning guards the porch.

That day, Renisha pressed her face hard
to the blinds and Lightning woke the house.

When a bloodhound says go, you go.
And then there was no more Renisha.

Blood, pink lotion, hair grease—spilling
from the bullet wound of an entire body.

He shot her—called her a bitch
because what else? The whole thing got too
messy and he was so mad that she stained his porch.

The Summer We All Stayed Alive

God was new to being God and needed help. Noah
was a patient man. He obeyed—chopped the trees down,

waited for God to tell him to stop. *This is a big boat*,
explained God. *You will save the deer, the chicken,*

the antelope, my precious things, explained God.
Noah killed trees for centuries. He kept going

even when he grew so old, rigor mortis stiffened
his long beard. Noah was a ride-or-die,

walked the earth to place his thumbprint on
the rescued heads, the valued hooves. Noah felt

the water rotting all around him
even though God did not say it was time.

Noah could not wait on God—he wanted to survive.
Cue: "Wade in the Water" // Cue: "Ride On, King Jesus."

Noah did not know who Jesus was but a storm
was coming and he was black, so he had to believe.

This is about staying alive. Noah says *fuck the ark*.
The animals light the holy wood on fire

for a barbecue. *We havin' the biggest block party*
on the planet. They bring their play-cousins and

aunties. The antelope are playing spades. The deer—
drinking Hennessy. The chickens are braiding

hair in the back. The chicken is also fried.
"Electric Slide" in the deep cauldron of the apocalypse.

The air is charcoal and Sweet Baby Ray's for so long
Noah almost thinks this summer can last forever, that

he and his niggas can outrun water, that the absence
of trees meant they could not be lynched?

Call a Funeral Home, or A Dead Body Can't Stay in This Room Overnight, or The First Thing We Need to Do Is Discard the IV Bags

Tantie Annette dies in her sleep and we circle the mattress, praying on our knees with heads covered in damp cloth. No one lowers the thermostat—we sweat through the carpet. No one lowers the thermostat, and Tantie Annette bakes. Bone marrow cooking through the cancerous skin. A colon sliding beneath a nightgown. I am asked to say the Rosary while my mother loops a scarf around Tantie's jaw—swinging shutters in an empty room // strange noose that double-knots the neck. *She can't stay here. She should be embalmed. Call a funeral home. Call 911.* My aunts pray until they say the spirit has left the room. Soaked in sweat, soaked in rain—they pull the saltwater dresses over their heads, replace them with bone-dry T-shirts. The bedside nurse tells us that a dead body can't stay in this room overnight—that we have to choose a funeral home before the organs curdle and leak. *Changes we wouldn't want to see.* We kiss her bloated head one by one. Medics fold Tantie into a bag. We cry in the boiling room. A window seals itself shut.

Vaughn

i

You opened up like a well-oiled fire hydrant when I told you
about the child you snuck inside of me like a secret
and I did not know what to do. With all of the roaches
and cigarette butts on the living room floor, you could
have made a swamp of the place. Do you think
about that sometimes? That your body can make
an ocean of itself, if only you just ask it to push?

ii

I'm writing an ode to everything I lost
in this apartment when you were my boyfriend:

my keys
a baby, the size of six purple grapes
my keys
my mind
my motherfucking ——

iii

The medicine grated at me until my insides were minced.
You could have poured my baby over pasta.

iv

The medicine boils a heap of mud inside of me.
My thighs blooming in red. The stillbirth
that sings through me like a child in the middle

of the sea. You leave me for a woman so clean,
she is a sonogram pinned to a white refrigerator.
You say her name like it is an indictment on your future.
You say it again and sound exhausted,
but I know tired and you aren't there yet.
I know because I watch how you pray
in the morning. Always for the same things
in the same order. You whistle along with
the kettle in the room. You laugh and
all of the birds fall out of the sky.
Let me iron your clothes. Let me
wash your dishes. Let me pretend.
Let me pretend. Let me. Let me.
Let me. Let me. Let me. Let me.
Please don't leave me here with
a mouth full of feathers and the blood
of every dead bird in the Midwest lopped
off in my mouth.

v

Do you have access to a gun?

Do you?

vi

[The first time I try to kill myself after the abortion it is an ordinary day.]

On my back, I lie. Stretched out on the kitchen floor,
I begged for thin blood and a reason for God to forgive.

I begged until the ambulance rolled up on me.
The fat sound of a siren in my ear,
the police, like roaches, all up in my shit,
crawling across my wrist for a pulse.
You run in to save me. You stand over
my body like how I imagine a chandelier
must stand over a ballroom it used to own.

vii

I was beautiful, once.
If I hold still, I can remember.
Yesterday, I wrote this with an extension
cord around my neck. *I forgive you*, I say
to myself in the mirror four times
before I claw the lie out of my fucking face.

viii

My fucking face, Vaughn.
Do you remember?

Flex

i. Flex

In a steaming dance hall, we throw money at Fatima's belly.
Dollar whine. Basement steeped in rum. Fatima's waist splits her
dress down the middle like a hot bake. The kind of pressure that cooks
water. Baby Daddy spins her in a circle. He kisses her with a mouth
full of curry. Spit the color of mop water, and we are pulling endless dollars
from our ribs. Over the speakers, Mad Cobra sings *ooman flex*.
Fatima cuts her knees over the money-green dance floor. Little girls
scoop the twenties under their can-can skirts—hoarding the bills
like hard candies from a piñata. Inside of her, a baby pounds
its head against the mortar. Faux locs leak saltwater down her greased scalp,
and we are pelting coins at her ankles. Copper shaking the room, like rain.
Twenty girls mouth *flex* and a river of glittering eggs spills from the hem
of Fatima's skirt. Blood memory: room-temperature molasses caked
on the wall. All of us circling the toilet where the head
of a guppy presses itself thin, and out of a teenaged body. The neck
of a half-formed son seeping through Fatima's gym shorts. But today,
we press our noses to the floor to sip her sap. Horse mouths bowed
to the good water.

ii. Fish Head

She swallows horse pills and the fish head
plops face down in toilet water. We all put our money
up for this—Foot Locker and Subway checks stacked
for weeks. Internet meds shipped in an opaque
box. Pseudonym where Fatima's name should be.
Unremarkable October sun. We skipped what the school
called the *biggest* track meet of the year, but cross-country was
white girl season anyway. Our brown and black legs archived
only for sprints. We locked the bathroom door in an empty house.

Fatima's thick thighs clenched over a mud-red toilet.
Crazy blood pools over her shit like gravy. Internet
pills even raze the bowels, but we are girls and ready to ride-
or-die. When she passes out, two of us drag her heavy body
to the bathtub. Skidmarks slug over porcelain. We turn the cool faucet
over her blue lips. We tie her head in a satin scarf and plastic
bag to save her hair.

iii. Rinse

Hunter says he will eat my pussy only if I let him fuck, to which I say
    word which
really means *I agree* and not *yes*. But OK, *word*. Virginity Pact of 2008—
    which may
sound like we were trying to preserve what was mostly fingered and not
    ran through.

But nah—
        in the spirit of exactitude: *We Gotta Practice on Something* Pact
        of 2008.
Word.

Hunter orders one carton of pork fried rice
and two Arizona iced teas. The half-chewed
grains slip from his teeth like maggots across
my neck. He locks the bathroom door in the
near-empty house. He shares a bunkbed with
his little brother, who is asleep with the lights
on. Chris Brown on repeat. *take you down   girl*

quit playin' baby girl   i'm gonna take   you down
                                                  baby baby baby baby baby

Word.

Dry pussy. Uneaten and dripping
something taffy-thick. Tap water between my legs
and I rinse and I rinse and I—

iv. So Fucking Grimy

Hunter's shit got you   walkin' funny girl   hey I got tampons in my bag
    if

anything, I got you   that nigga is corny   he supposed to   get it
    wet first

wtf?   he hit you with it like that?   oh nah.   sis   he's wyling

I know that nigga's older sister   we could squad up   on him

like now. like whenever.   WOW   he SO fucking grimy   damn for real?

hey, I got extra gym shorts on me too   it's red, but not *red red*
    can't notice it 'less you

get real close. you got a sweater or something?   OK, wrap it around your
    waist *like this*   just act

like it's your period   so fucked up   it's not supposed to hurt OD like that

you said *yes* or *no*?   OK word   at least he got the C-Breezy for you   LOL

whatever, girl   we got your back   you let him bust in you too, the fuck?
    damn

damn OK   lemme go to my locker real quick   I got you on some gym
    shorts
after sixth-period lunch.

Hennypalooza

after Jay-Z's "U Don't Know"
after Kanye West's "Take One for the Team"
for Michele

Me and my homegirl Michele wear dresses made of suede—
our braids swayed waist-length against the current of niggas fiending and
    fawning

at the wedge of our black stiletto heels. No. Our shoes are not bloody
and we smell like ghetto-bitch in the key of "Love Spell." We drink a fifth
    of Henny

all to ourselves. My unabridged mouth covers the neck of the glass bottle
that I pass with my left to my right hand. She holds both my hands in
    the club

when my schizophrenia pivots its ugly head against the epileptic
strobe lights. A rapper on stage screams into the mic: *They ain't know I
    had the Glock*

now everybody gettin' shot. Everybody gettin' shot and the ricochet sounds
real in my head,
so I dive underneath the beat. My palms clap both my ears like two gold
    plates

of a cymbal. Wore two gold plates like a sex symbol. But I feel cheap
in my Instagram dress. So much coke in me, my blood could

run the slalom. I remember the suicide note I keep
in my purse and I sink into the dance floor. My knees buckling

to the tune of "Dutty Wine." Tony Matterhorn: the discography
of my personal apocalypse. I dance until there is no more water

left in this body. Until there is no more self-harm left
in my little body. I dance until all the men fall out of this body.

But there is one name that I can't shake, not even with the weight
of my hips. I call him from the bathroom, higher than I've ever been.

His voice is sturdy like the floorboards in a Catholic church. He is bored
with my unoriginal tears and the mental illness—my perforated brain.

Later on he fucks me as charity, and I feel ashamed.
Low as I am, Michele lifts my chin with her finger to the sky.

Heads high. Kill him with it. Kill him with it. Kill him with it.
She sings until I smile. She love every tooth in my blunted-up mouth.

She love every earned nap in my tender head.

Acknowledgments

I would like to thank the following journals for giving my work a home:

Apogee: "Raw Video Footage"

The BreakBeat Poets Black Girl Magic Anthology: "Love and Water"

The Offing: "Some Girls Survive on Their Sorcery Alone"

The Rumpus: "Rinse" (from "Flex")

7 Mag: "The Summer We All Stayed Alive"

Winter Tangerine: "slickmouth"

Thank you to my family, my friends, my ancestors, and greatest teachers:

Anika Dottin, Geo, Juliet James, Felicia Magnan, Nabila Lovelace, Michele St. Julien, Zane Rudolfo, Yolanda Pruitt, Sofia Snow, Cassy Marzette, Lorena Barbosa, Jayson P. Smith, Cydney Edwards, Jehanne Belange, Thierry Thompson, Danez Smith, Christian Eatman, Mama and Papa Eatman, Amarah Salgado, Prolific, Natalie Ciara Cook, Karl Iglesias, Jared Morgan, Will Giles, Ada Umubera, Ashley Thomas, Jordan Shafah Gaines, Richard Lance Jones, Layla Jones, Gretchen Carvajal, Brianna Johnson, Perla Lozoya, Bobbie Briggs, Nneka Akubeze, Jess X Snow, Desiree C. Bailey, Jasmine Magnan, Angela Thompson, Asia Adean-Torres, Lucy Osakwe, Elton Ferdinand III, Zhalarina Sanders, Shanyce Spain, Zechariah Ruffin, Taneisha Broadway, Ajanae Dawkins, P'fanique Hill, Mionna Short, Najee Ritter, Sean B, Sarah Barnes, Sarah Bruno, Emma Bracy, Nia Scott, Tasia Morgan, Diamond Colvin,

Tanay Semple, Chika Onwuvuche, Brielle James, Jay Katelansky, Janell Humphrey, Hiwot Adilow, Malcolm Halsey-Milhaupt, Eli Lynch, Ricardo Cortez de la Cruz II, Mariam Coker, Sam Arriozola, Leslie Sainz, Alisha Dietzman, Carolyn Orosz, Dylan Weir, Diamond Forde, Sammie Scott, Troizel Carr, Shyiah Trotman, Hannah Oberman-Breindel, Rafael Casal, Chris Walker, Ms. Fedus, Ms. Williams, Ishmael Islam, Blue Bellinger, Gethsemane Herron, Carvens Lissaint, Diamond Howard, Lo Anderson, Jasmine Mans, Ajay Johnson, Yena Purmasir ,Shiyah Trotman, Adey Assefa, Amaris Diaz, Chanel Dupree, Kearah Armonie, Shawn Harris, Meaca Moore, Dominique Ricks, Ittai Wong, Dominic Masaki, Jill Fukumoto, Steven Rodriguez, Myriha Burton, Ashlyn Akins, Ashley Street, Adam Levin, Alida Cardos Whaley, Blaire White, Candance Thompson, Danielle Tootsie-Watson, Jonah Mixon-Webster, Wilfred Ruck, Julian Randall, Matthew Hall-Ming, Shynah James, Beatrice Huttner, Aurora Mausam-Javed, Jasmine Noel Calvin, Paige Ali Lewis, Amani-Breanna Alexander, Alia Pope, Serit Kelly, Sydney Phillips, DeLana R.A. Dameron, Amanda Woodington, Xavier Green, Naajidah Correll, Janel Herrera, Barbara Gonzalez, Jasmine Savoy, Joanna Romero, Casey Coulson, Kiana Murphy, Rachel McKibbens, Jerriod Avant, Jeremy Michael Clark, Gabriel Ramirez, Michael Penn II, Kimanh Truong, Christian Robinson, Sean Medlin, Amy Reidel, Marvel Myrtile, Dr. Leah Mirakhor, Ms. Hazel, Deejay Reborn, Dr. Mary Layoun, Garrett Pauli, Nia Allan Lee, Hugh Hunter, Andrea and Bill Scarborough, Paul Tran, Taren Mansfield, Erika Dickerson, Nina Lydia Hassan Koroma, Lola Omolabi, Cartecia Lawrence, Rachel Ann Stotts, Dionna Nicole James-Jones, Aliyah Muhammad, Trace De Passe, Cindy Tran, Jasmine Reid, Haydil Henriquez, Sarah Passino, Sebastien Bernard, Sokunthary Svay, Moncho Alvarado, Joel Diaz, Aracelis Girmay, Amy Quan Barry, Ronald Wallace, Sean Bishop, Amaud Johnson, Jesse Lee Kercheval, Nurse Mike, Erica Mariam Fabri, George Wilson, Auntie Marcia, Auntie Pam, Auntie Judy, Auntie Patsy, Auntie Michele, Auntie Margaret, Auntie Dianne, Auntie Ava, Auntie Jackie, Auntie DD, Auntie Gemma, Auntie Paula, Auntie Marcia Wilson, Auntie Angela, Uncle Busta, Uncle Steven, Uncle David, Uncle Huey, Uncle Charlie, Uncle Bert, Uncle Wayne, Uncle Wayne Morgan, Uncle Bill, Auntie

Dallison, Auntie Maud, Auntie Sandra Dottin, Ria, Jayden Jones, Ayinka Carrington, Anton Carrington, Surraya Carrington, Naima Carrington, Tsara Gittens, Sonja Ottley, Meghan Burkett, Michael Burkett, Kamilah Alexander, Jermaine Alexander, Danah Solomon, Chenelle Dasent, Chikera Nurse, Zerzura Nurse, Brett Lucas, Nori, Jax, Jeremiah, Granny Florence, Calaloo 2015 (Brown University), Pink Door 2016, The Zeta Xi Core Chapter of Delta Sigma Theta, Incorporated (AOML), Granny Juanita, Auntie Ann Marie, Andrew Thomas, Nakila Robinson, John Vietnam, thank you to "P-Unit": my mother Andrea E.C. Nurse and my father Gregory E. Brathwaite (I love you for keeping me alive), thank you to everyone at Northwestern University Press. Thank you to all those who read this little book. Thank you God.

Thiahera Nurse is from Hollis, Queens, by way of Trinidad and Tobago. She received her M.F.A. in poetry at the University of Wisconsin–Madison. Her work can be found in *The Rumpus*, *Callaloo*, *The Offing*, and in the forthcoming edition of *The BreakBeat Poets Anthology*. She has received support from *Callaloo*, *Tin House*, and The Pink Door Writing Retreat. She is a 2018 Poets House Emerging Poets Fellow. She writes for the black girls (the living and the dead).